T-6 TEXAN

T-6 TEXAN

THE IMMORTAL PILOT TRAINER

WILLIAM JESSE

Acknowledgements

A book of this nature could never have been compiled without the help of many people and organizations. I would like to thank the following individuals and associations: Bob Kennedy; Bob James of Merritt Island, Florida; Bill Klaers out at Rialto, California; the Valiant Air Command; Jacques Lacombe; Pat Hanna and the Canadian Harvard Aircraft Association; Tom Smith of Sarasota; Jim Dent and his R4D-8; Patsy Hagler down in Breckenridge; Jerry O'Neill; Jeff Ethell; and many others who I will mention within the book. The photographs in this volume were taken with Canon equipment loaded with either Kodachrome 25 or 64 slide film.

Published in 1991 by Osprey Publishing Limited
59 Grosvenor Street, London W1X 9DA

© William Jesse 1991

British Library Cataloguing in Publication Data
Jesse, William
  T-6 Texans, Harvards and SNJs.
  1. United States. Military aircraft
  I. Title
  623.74620973

ISBN 1-85532-154-8

Editor Tony Holmes
Page design by Paul Kime
Printed in Hong Kong

Front cover A pristine pair. Maintaining perfect formation over a thick belt of cloud, a sparkling deuce of SNJ-5s from the *Six of Diamonds* display team close in on the author's camera ship. Like many T-6s still flying today, the aircraft closest to the camera has no windshield framing fitted

Back cover The distinctive unit insignia of the 111th Fighter Squadron, 147th Fighter Group, based at Ellington Field in Houston in 1941. The marking is proudly worn by a Texas-based AT-6A

Title page The Harvard is a big aeroplane, possessing a fuselage length of 29 ft and a wing-span of 42 ft, the latter being greater than that of the Mustang, Spitfire or Hurricane. Yet it has about half the horsepower of these fighters. As a trainer it could punish as quickly as it could reward, the unwritten law stating that once a pilot qualified in a Harvard, he could qualify in any aircraft

For a catalogue of all books published by Osprey Aerospace
please write to:

The Marketing Department,
Octopus Illustrated Books, 1st Floor, Michelin House,
81 Fulham Road, London SW3 6RB

William Jesse has been involved in aviation since the late 1960s, his love of aircraft, especially older ones, and his interest in photography, having led him to publish many aviation articles over the years. He considers himself very fortunate to have flown in more than 100 different types of aircraft, with the T-6 Texan undoubtedly being his favourite. William currently lives in Montreal, not far from the noise of the aircraft at Dorval Airport.

Introduction

Undoubtedly the most famous trainer of World War 2, the North American Aviation Company's T-6 Texan was developed to meet the requirements of a United States Army Air Corps Basic Trainer competition held in 1935. North American called their design the NA-16, although it would become known throughout its lifetime by many other names and model numbers. It became the world's most popular and versatile single-engined training aircraft, more than 21,000 aeroplanes being built by North American, and under licence in four countries. The Army Air Corps was not alone in choosing the Texan as its new trainer, the US Navy soon realizing its potential and adapting the design to its needs, calling their version the SNJ. Canadian and British forces also obtained the aircraft, naming their version the Harvard, with a large number of these being built under licence in Canada.

The NA-16, and its variants, served with many of the world's air forces, and was responsible for the training of hundreds of thousands of American and Allied airmen. It was a veteran of three wars, and on some occasions, armed with rockets and machine guns, saw service as a light combat aircraft.

After World War 2, large numbers of Texans were either sold to foreign armed forces or disposed of on the civilian market. Initially too expensive to operate privately as sport planes, T-6s were used as skywriters, crop dusters, mail carriers and air racers throughout the 1950s and 60s. A spate of epic war films in the late 1960s and early 70s also saw the T-6 become a Hollywood film star, the humble trainer performing admirably as an A6M Zero in *Tora, Tora, Tora* and *Baa, Baa, Blacksheep*.

Today, more than 50 years after the design came off the drawing boards at North American Aviation, these aircraft are still highly visible. Some are used by the South African Air Force, many are still flown in air races, but most are seen in the warbird movement. The staple performer at many an airshow, the venerable T-6/Harvard is a firm favourite with aviation enthusiasts the world over, its relative simplicity ensuring that more and more 'Pilot Makers' appear on the civil registers every year.

Right The Harvards in use with the Royal Canadian Navy (RCN) did not see the same amount of service as their brothers in the Air Force. After the war the RCN used the aircraft primarily to train Seafire pilots. They were not carrier-based, nor did they have tail-hooks as did some models of the SNJ. However, some of the west coast-based aircraft did wear rudder stripes

Contents

T-6 Texan

The Texan was one of the most important aircraft ever designed. Given the North American Aviation model number NA-16, it flew just six weeks after the initial design specifications were submitted and approved by the Army. Although the NA-16 was progressively modified over its ten-year production run, the basic design of the aircraft remained essentially the same. It became in turn the BT-9 and the BT-14 (BT standing for Basic Trainer), the BC-1 (for Basic Combat) and the AT-6 (for Advanced Trainer); North American Aviation's own factory codes changed even more frequently depending on modifications, minor or major, to the airframe or to the customer's needs. The first aircraft was delivered to the 36th Pursuit Squadron at Mitchell Field, Long Island, in 1940. Call it the Texan, the 'Pilot Maker' or even the 'Yellow Peril', it was the proven basic training aircraft of many air arms, and although it was never an easy aeroplane to master, it was a true teacher. To a budding young fighter pilot, the T-6 was an excellent stepping stone on to the high performance types that were to follow in his career. A familiar sight in the skies over Texas during the 1940s and early 1950s, these T-6s recreate history as they maintain an impeccable formation over the parched rural scrubland of the 'Lone Star' state. The aircraft closest to the camera wears the USAF Training Command emblem on its cowling (*Bob Kennedy*)

Because of the sheer size of the T-6 production run (15,109 built by North American Aircraft alone), the aircraft has survived to become the most populous warbird in the world today. A nice steady platform for formation flying, the rasping Texan is the mount of several demonstration teams in the USA. Benefitting from a small dose of diesel fuel injected into their exhausts, these Texans trail a plume of white smoke across the sky, giving their performance that 'Thunderbirds' feeling!

Right A blue fuselage with yellow wings was the standard Army Air Force trainer scheme up to 1940 when a bare metal finish became standard. However, seeing that this particular aircraft is actually a T-6G, it seems unlikely that it would have worn the blue scheme at any point in its service career

Above As a result of the American National Security Act of 1947 the Air Force finally became independent of the Army, and accordingly it removed the Army designations from its aircraft. The A for Advanced was removed from the AT-6 and it became simply the T-6

Right The T-6G was the last major variant of the Texan produced, North American remanufacturing aircraft using available airframes from earlier versions. Changes included an improved cockpit with updated radios, a modified hydraulic system, an increase in fuel capacity, a modified undercarriage with a steerable Mustang-type tailwheel, and a square-tipped propeller with spinner. The most noticeable modification was the canopy, where several of the metal frames were removed, thereby improving visibility. Some 2068 'new' T-6Gs were built in four locations—Downey, Fresno and Long Beach, all in California, and Columbus, Ohio. Although all T-6Gs were painted trainer yellow, other schemes were worn once the aircraft reached squadron service. The T-6G was phased out of the Air Force inventory in 1958

Below Instituted in the 1950s by the armed forces, the 'buzz number' coding on the fuselage was aimed specifically at low flying pilots who enjoyed 'beating up' bases and communities in their aircraft. Consisting of a pair of letters and three numbers carried on the fuselage sides and under the left wing, the 'buzz' code gave harassed citizens the opportunity to identify those guilty of such feats. For T-6s the letter T identified the aircraft as a trainer, with the A referring specifically to the Texan. The three numbers were the last three digits of its Air Force serial

Above Steadily climbing into a murky overcast, the pilot tucks the gear away on his pristine LT-6G. Assigned to the Maryland Air National Guard at some point in its life, this particular Texan is finished in a typical early 1950s ANG scheme. An integral part of the 'Guard in the 1950s, the T-6s acted as proficiency flying trainers for most units, sharing ramp space with fighters and transports alike

Right Wearing a curious blend of faded markings, an anonymous T-6G taxies out towards the runway. Judging from its external appearance, this particular aircraft may have just been restored to an airworthy condition

Below In marked contrast, this T-6G positively gleams, the highly polished finish of its fuselage revealing the stress-riveted construction of the Texan. The more common ADF (Automatic Direction-Finder) loop fairing has been replaced in this case by a more modern looking blade aerial, this modification perhaps better reflecting the standard of the radio equipment fitted in this particular aircraft

Left Many Texans are painted up in colours not entirely representative of the schemes they wore when they served with the USAF. This particular aircraft wears an unusual drab olive green finish, although the weathering of the paint just above the wheel-well reveals the original trainer yellow factory finish underneath

Above Is this particular T-6 'a dog of an aeroplane to fly', or does it handle like Snoopy's kennel perhaps? Either way, you can bet the pilot's name is Schultz!

Right Wearing white diamonds on its tail (a marking associated with the air wing embarked aboard USS *Essex* (CV-9) in 1944/45), and an overall gloss sea blue finish on its fuselage and wings, this particular T-6G looks more like a naval fighter of World War 2 rather than a USAAF Trainer from the same period

Right Powered by a Pratt & Whitney R-1340-AN-1 engine, and having a wing gun and bomb racks installed, the AT-6B proved to be slightly more potent than the preceding AT-6A. Painted in the markings of JG 54 (Green Hearts), Dick Sykes' Texan sports a finish that would appear to be equally at home on a Messerschmitt Bf 109

Below The Condor Squadron in Van Nuys, California, could easily be called a flying museum, its members operating a fleet of T-6s and SNJs painted in American and German markings. Flown regularly, the aircraft are called upon to perform search and rescue missions in the Van Nuys area

Previous pages A closer look at another member of the Condor Squadron reveals the quality of the finished paintwork on the unit's fleet of T-6s. Texans and Harvards have often 'changed sides' for the sake of Hollywood, and its celluloid portrayal of World War 2

Above Who said Texans can't fly fast!? Dick Sykes' AT-6B set a new Texan/SNJ course record of 225.943 mph at Reno in 1983. A total of 1400 AT-6Bs were built at North American's Dallas plant, these machines operating primarily as gunnery trainers with a Browning .30 calibre machine gun mounted in the starboard wing. The Bravo model was also capable of carrying up to four 100lb bombs in special underwing racks

Right A well-used member of the Condor Squadron, this T-6 shows signs of being run on an over rich mixture of fuel, the rather imaginative camouflage scheme beginning to melt near the exhaust stub

Above It is usually a safe bet to say that at least one T-6 painted in Luftwaffe markings will turn up at every American airshow, this rather conservatively coloured machine belonging to a colonel in the Confederate Air Force. In the 1950s the re-born Luftwaffe took delivery of a large quantity of Canadian Car and Foundry (CCF)-built T-6Js (Harvard Mk IVs), these aircraft being purchased with American aid money made available through the auspices of the Mutual Defense Assistance Program (MDAP)

Above right Due to an Army Air Corps re-evaluation of aircraft in the basic combat category, the formerly designated BC-1A Texans became AT-6s, thus reflecting the change in the aircraft's overall mission to that of an advanced trainer. It was re-engined with a Pratt & Whitney 600 hp R-1340-47 radial engine and provisions were made for a Browning .30 calibre gun mounted in the rear cockpit

Below right The AT-6A was basically the same as the AT-6, but powered by a 600 hp R-1340-49 engine and featuring, among other items, removable wing centre section fuel tanks. This Texan is painted as the 41st airframe delivered to the Air Corps, and it wears the markings of the 111th Fighter Squadron, 147th Fighter Group, based at Ellington Field in Houston during 1941. It was photographed in 1990 while participating in the Breckenridge airshow, a major event held annually in Texas

Above There is a long rebuild ahead for this California-based AT-6F. Simple welded steel tubing in separate sub-assemblies for the engine area, the centre section and rear fuselage, all bolted together to form the Texan airframe. The wing outer panels attached to the centre section, and to facilitate maintenance, the metal alloy fuselage skins could be easily removed

Right Like all Texans from the AT-6B onwards, the T-6F version was powered by the nine-cylinder Pratt & Whitney R-1340-AN-1 engine. Prop spinners also became standard on this model, but mechanics servicing the hubs in the field often found the job easier if the spinner was left off. The small rear-view mirror in the cockpit is not for spotting enemy aircraft approaching from the six o'clock, but to check on the well being of the passenger 'back aft'!

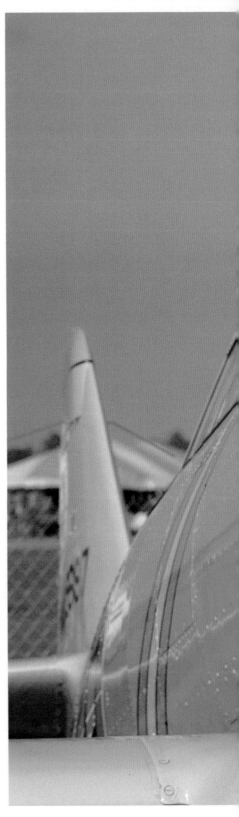

Left In the mid-1950s Japan acquired a significant fleet of Harvards and Texans from Britain and the United States. Howard Pardue, an owner of many radial-engined US Navy aircraft, also possesses an AT-6, painted more like a Zero than a post-war Japanese training aircraft!

Below The Japanese actually utilized up to 176 T-6s as pilot trainers during World War 2, the Allied forces assigning the aircraft the code-name 'Oak'. However, the actual authenticity of this scheme is open to some conjecture

Many Texans are still airworthy the world over but few could rival the overall finish of this beautifully restored AT-6D, sprayed up in authentic USAF training colours. The owner has even gone as far as to apply authentic serials to the appropriate fuselage panels and brand new Hamilton Standard decals to the prop blades

The Spanish Air Force was a late recipient of the Texan, the first T-6s arriving in 1954. The T-6Ds they received were called C.6s, the letter designation standing for *Caza*, or fighter. These aircraft were armed with Browning .30 calibre wing guns and underwing hardpoints, and were used for light strike duties and forward air control (FAC). Most of the C.6s had a metallic finish, although a number of T-6Gs were delivered as trainers and designated E.16s, these aircraft wearing a more traditional yellow scheme. Aircraft 421-50 served with *Escuadron* 421, one of the last Spanish units to use the Texan, and is one of the 30 or so aircraft that were retired by the Spanish and returned to the United States in the early 1980s. It would be nice to see some of these repatriated aircraft retain their Spanish Air Force markings

Above Phased out of regular Air Force service in 1958, surplus Texans were then taken on charge by the Civil Air Patrol (CAP). Based at Van Nuys, this aircraft is still used by the CAP and has been involved in more than 20 successful search and rescue missions. The tinted green upper canopy panels (never seen in USAF service) offer some relief from the warm California sun

Above left The AT-6D was virtually identical to the preceding AT-6C except for the fact that its electrical generator was a 24-volt system compared to the Charlie model's 12. A grand total of 3958 AT-6Ds were built by North American, 440 of them with moulded three-ply mahogany plywood rear fuselage assemblies

Below left Leaving the fuselage unpainted usually means a lot of polishing for somebody. The owner of this Aspen, Colorado, based Texan has opted to paint the fuselage of his aircraft an aluminium colour to save him having to continually perform this onerous chore

Above Today, Texans still race around the pylons at Reno. A fun hobby if you can afford it, some owners defray the costs of operating T-6s by offering their aircraft as 200-mph billboards, this particular Texan being sponsored by the American Dairy Queen chain

Left An aggressor T-6D perhaps? A veteran from another era, this Texan takes on a 1990's appearance with a wrapround scheme complete with low-viz 'star and bar'. This particular Texan wears a Valiant Air Command crest just behind the engine air intake

Above Yet another spurious scheme adorns this T-6D. The style of radio antenna fitted to this particular airframe is also rather curious, whilst the large '93' sprayed on just behind the cowling suggests that the aircraft has recently competed in a Reno Air Race meeting

Left Compared to some of the other Texans illustrated in this volume, this poor old T-6F looks positively knackered. Still wearing a faded 'star and bar' on the fuselage, the aircraft was spotted languishing in amongst the hangars at Chino Airport, near Los Angeles. The last production variant of the Texan family, less than 1000 T-6Fs were built by North American. Restored back to pure training configuration, the F- model had all its armament deleted and the bomb racks removed. However, it was capable of carrying an external 20-gallon fuel tank on the fuselage centreline aft of the main wheel wells

Above Ninety miles per hour and flaps at 45 degrees. Now comes what most pilots consider the most difficult part of flying a T-6—keeping the aircraft straight after touchdown. The Texan's reputation for ground looping after landing was notorious, so consequently the most commonly replaced part of the aircraft was its wing tips. Just to make things worse, the flap and gear handles were located near each other, so it was not unusual for a new pilot to pull the wrong handle and land with the wheels retracted

Right The cockpit of a T-6 could be likened to the cockpit of most World War 2 fighters, although it is somewhat roomier than the 'office' of a P-51 Mustang or a Spitfire

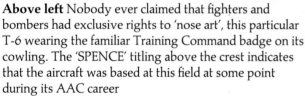

Above left Nobody ever claimed that fighters and bombers had exclusive rights to 'nose art', this particular T-6 wearing the familiar Training Command badge on its cowling. The 'SPENCE' titling above the crest indicates that the aircraft was based at this field at some point during its AAC career

Above right One of the major improvements built into the definitive Texan was a fully retractable undercarriage, this modification to the early BT-family of trainers better reflecting the modern trend in fighter design. First flown in the prototype BC-1 on 11 February 1938, the retractable undercarriage, together with the more powerful R-1340-47 version of the venerable Wasp engine, gave the BC-1 a 19-mph advantage over the earlier BTs, the former's top speed peaking at 209 mph

Right A rearward view from the cockpit of Andy Michalak's Oshkosh Reserve Grand Champion-winning Maryland Air National Guard T-6G. The flat housing behind the canopy replaced the football-shaped ADF antenna enclosure of earlier models. Close attention to detail is a determining factor in deciding a prize winning aircraft, hence the stencilling on the rear seat pack harness. The folded white curtain tucked into the rear of the cockpit is the instrument training hood which unfolded over the student during IFR (Instrument Flying Rules) training

Harvard

When the British government established the Empire Air Training Scheme at the outset of World War 2, they found themselves without a suitable training aircraft. With their own industries concentrating on combat types, the British looked to the United States to fill their needs. Impressed with the North American Yale, the British placed an order with the company for an advanced trainer based on the BC-1 (a two-seat aircraft with a fabric covered rear fuselage), and similar to the BT-9 but featuring a retractable landing gear. They named the aircraft the Harvard Mk I. In place of the 550 hp Pratt & Whitney engine on the BC-1, the British order specified a 600 hp Pratt & Whitney R-1340-S3H1. The Harvard was built over the years in four marks and was utilized by many air forces including the RAF, the RCAF, the RNZAF and the *Armée de l'Air*. A large number of these Harvards were built in Canada by Noorduyn Aviation and its successor, Canadian Car and Foundry (CCF), whilst other countries such as Sweden, Australia and even Japan built versions of the aircraft under licence. In the 1950s, many Mk IVs were furnished to embryonic NATO air forces. Production of the Harvard ended in the mid-1950s at the CCF plant in Fort William, Ontario. Looking even better than when it left the CCF factory 40 years ago, this prize winning Harvard IV is now owned by Bill Melamed. Awarded a first at Oshkosh in 1989, the aircraft has caused many a T-6 owner to kick the tyres of his aircraft in frustration after seeing the beauty up close

Above Wearing the serial AJ583, this aircraft was part of an order for Harvard IIs placed by the *Armée de l'Aire* that was taken over by Britain just before France fell to the Germans in June 1940. It was completed to Harvard II standards and delivered as such, eventually joining the RCAF in 1944 when the British Training Scheme ended in Canada, leaving it, and many others, behind. Although officially RCAF property, it still retained its RAF serial number

Right The RCAF obtained their Harvards from various sources, the first Mk IIs being pulled from a batch ordered by the British government. Aircraft 3222 was part of a second order for Mk IIs placed by Britain on behalf of the RCAF. In January 1940, the RCAF placed their own order for 210 Mk IIB aircraft (licence-built by Noorduyn), and another 1500 Mk IIBs were ordered by the US Government on behalf of the RCAF under the lend-lease programme

Below Belonging to the Canadian Harvard Aircraft Association (CHAA) and photographed in June 1987, this Mk II was repainted during the winter of 1988 in its original Empire Training scheme. Cold Canadian winters offer Harvard owners the chance to rebuild in anticipation of the finer weather to come

Left The Harvard was finally retired from the RCAF in May 1965, having served from July 1939. Throughout its career, the aircraft had been responsible for the training of some 19,000 airmen (*Pat Hanna*)

Left Thirty six inches of manifold pressure for full power, lift off and quickly back to 30 inches and 2000 RPM for climb out while the airport gradually falls away. Some Harvard Mk IVs were built without landing gear doors, and it is widely believed that only those aircraft made by CCF for export under the MDAP were actually provided with such luxuries

Above The Canadian Harvards differed in several respects from their brethren flying 'south of the border' in the USA. One of the more visible differences centred around the aircraft's exhaust stub, the Noorduyn and CCF Harvards having an extended shroud fitted to the 'pipeworks' to channel heated air from the engine into the frozen cockpit during winter operations. As I'm sure you can tell from the spotless finish, this close-up shot is of Bill Melamed's Harvard IV

The Harvard II was basically an 'anglicized' AT-6C, its heavily framed canopy contrasting markedly with the later Mk IV. This particular Harvard IIB wears the appropriate wartime scheme of overall gloss yellow, with period roundels and fin flash

Fred Websters's 1952 Harvard Mk IV is painted up to represent an aircraft from the RCAF's *Goldilocks* aerobatic team. From 1962 to 1964 the instructor-manned *Goldilocks* flew what could best be described as a comedy formation routine, inspired by the antics of their students

Left Compared to the traditional tri-colour fin flashes, the post-war tail markings applied to the Harvard fleet were a rather radical departure from the norm. I would hate to have been the poor aircraftsman who had to hand paint the crests on every Harvard in RCAF service at the time of the switch over!

Below It's just a case of getting out the stencil and the paint brushes in this case!

AJ583

LIFT HERE

Above Another view of the custom-made exhaust shroud fitted to Canadian Harvards. An effective system which worked exceptionally well, the Pratt & Whitney 'heater' made the Harvard's cockpit the ideal spot to be in on a cold winter's morning

Above Not all Harvard owners wanted a warbird, this Mk II looking very much like a sports aircraft until it was purchased by the CHAA in 1987. During the winter of 1988 it was completely stripped and repainted in the original service colours of a British Commonwealth Air Training Plan (BCATP) Harvard. During the rebuild, wing tip fences were replaced with the original tips and the prop spinner was removed (*Pat Hanna*)

Above left As one of the basic training aircraft types in the RCAF, the Harvard was a common sight in Canadian skies. Today, the aircraft is still popular in Canada, 44 appearing on the latest civil aircraft register

Below left During World War 2 New Zealand acquired 203 Mk II and Mk III Harvards from Great Britain and the United States, this particular aircraft, RNZAF 1085, being an ex-RAF Harvard III imported in 1944. Finally retired in June 1977, the Harvard has retained its Air Force colours and continues to fly on the civil register today. Two other ex-RNZAF aircraft also appear on the current New Zealand register

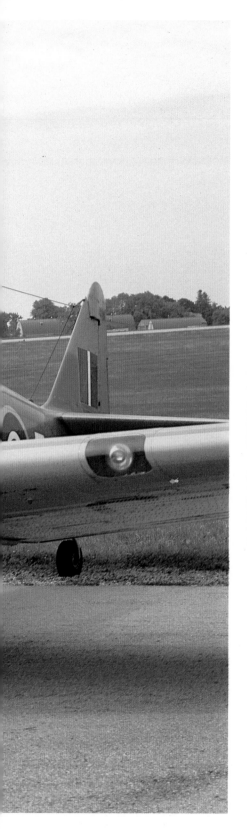

Left The biggest customer for the Harvard was the Royal Air Force who received their first aircraft from the North American plant in Inglewood, California. The first Mk I arrived at the Aeroplane & Armament Experimental Establishment, Martlesham Heath, England, in December 1938 to undergo flight trials. Used by many countries over the past 50 years, the Harvard is still in use today with the South African Air Force. Although there are examples of three marks flying today, unfortunately no Mk Is have been preserved. This Mk 4, nicknamed 'SLO-MO-SHUN', wears a rather strange tan and green scheme

Above Proudly flying the flag, this particular Harvard is well and truly 'bombed-up'

Above Well-worn, this Harvard II wears an authentic post-war RAF training command scheme of the 1950s. This photo could easily have been taken 40 years ago at any RAF station, most squadrons having at least one battered aircraft on strength operating as a unit 'hack'. Only the small 'N' code beneath its tailplane gives the ruse away, indicating that this Harvard appears on the US civil register

Right The USAF paid for 285 of the 555 Harvard IVs built by the CCF, and designated them T-6J-CCFs. These were built for MDAP countries, but six were used by the USAF as replacements for crashed T-6Ds. 'Sarge' is an ex-RCAF Harvard, minus the modified exhaust stack

SNJ

What the Texan was to the Army Air Force, the SNJ was to the Navy, their first experience with the North American Aviation Company's trainer coming in 1936 when they ordered a modified version of the BT-9. Designated the NJ-1, the aircraft had a fixed undercarriage, was fabric covered and, unsurprisingly, was a two-seater. One of the important qualifications specified by the Navy was that the aircraft had to use a powerplant that was already in service with its air arm. Accordingly, the Wright R-975 installed in the BT-9 was replaced by a Pratt & Whitney 500 hp R-1340 Wasp, turning a two-bladed controllable pitch propeller. Most of the NJ-1s were sent to Corry Field, Pensacola, where they served as instrument trainers. The SNJ-1, an all-metal aircraft with retractable landing gear, was acquired in 1938 when the Navy realized that they needed a high performance aircraft to train pilots to fly its new scout aeroplanes like the Douglas SBD and the Grumman Wildcat. The first SNJ-1s were delivered in May 1939 to NAS Anacostia. Only 16 SNJ-1s were built, and when the later SNJ-2s and -3s came on line, it was decided that the earlier airframes were too unlike the others to be of any use, the SNJ-1s being scrapped at the end of 1943. Obviously not an SNJ-1, this particular aircraft is in fact an SNJ-5, beautifully restored in its wartime colours

Left Part of the Navy requirement for the SNJ called for up-graded radios and enhanced salt water corrosion proofing. Later requirements saw a reinforced fuselage fitted to accept a tail-hook for carrier landing training, this distinctively 'blue water' feature appearing first on the SNJ-3, and then on all later models, the modification being installed by the Navy at Pensacola from 1942 onwards. The Navy was responsible for the complete re-fit, including the manufacture of the required parts. Over 270 SNJ-3s were built specifically to contract whilst an additional 296 were obtained from the USAAF, but of these only 12 were modified for carrier operations. Further versions of the SNJ family were acquired throughout the 1940s, but relatively few were fitted with tail hooks. Those that did, had the suffix -C added to their designation, this feature clearly setting them apart from both the Texan and the Harvard. Some SNJs were assigned to carriers, but were seldom taken on deployment. The landing gear doors on many of these aircraft were also removed, either intentionally or as a result of a rough landing. This SNJ-5C clearly shows its flimsy hook stowed securely beneath the fuselage. The mock Browning .30 machine gun mounting faired into the forward fuselage may have been fitted for 'celluloid' purposes

Above The designation SNJ was derived from SN for Scout Trainer and J for the code assigned by the Navy to North American Aviation. Like the Texan and the Harvard, the SNJ was built in various models over its lifespan, and often on the same assembly lines as the Air Force and British Commonwealth aircraft

Left The SNJ-3 and the AT-6A were identical aircraft. Although there were some differences between the Texan and the SNJ in later models, all aircraft from the SNJ-3 on were built on US Army contracts and then transferred to the Navy

Below There are few SNJ-2s remaining. The standard long range fuel tanks (190 gallons) made it a good cross-country trainer and today the aircraft does well as a skywriter, advertising for concerns like the The Miller Brewing Company. Distinguished by their flat-bottomed rudders and engine-mounted oil coolers, SNJ-2s are amongst the most highly prized members of the T-6/SNJ/Harvard family

Left The most numerous of the 'J-Birds' was the SNJ-4, 2401 being built to contract at the Dallas factory. Bill Klaers' aircraft is a very stock model, painted in the markings of the carrier USS *Lexington* (CV-16). Unlike Texans or Harvards, the SNJs were always brightly finished

Above Close-up detail of the unit insignia on Bill Klaers' SNJ-4. This aircraft wears the pre-war 1939/40 colour scheme of VB-2, the *Lexington's* embarked bomber unit. At the time, VB-2 flew the less than impressive SB2U-2 Vindicator, the squadron probably operating one or two SNJ-1s as proficiency trainers

Left Although advanced trainers for the Navy were delivered in a plain bare metal finish, once the aircraft entered squadron service its operational scheme could hardly be described as boring. The top sides of the wings were painted chrome yellow indicating the trainer role, whilst rudders, engine cowlings and wings tips were often painted in colours connected with the individual training units

Above Hank Moretti's SNJ-5 displays the simple, but effective, lines of the famous North American product. The distinctive skyward arrow on the fin of Hank's aircraft is modelled on the air wing badge worn by aircraft embarked on USS *Bunker Hill* (CV-17) during 1944/45

Overleaf In an effort to reduce the amount of precious aluminium used in the manufacture of training aircraft, North American redesigned the rear bulkheads, fuselage skins and tailplanes of later SNJ-4s and T-6Cs to incorporate plywood and spruce. This process offered a saving of nearly 200 pounds of aluminium per aircraft, even though the finished airframe was heavier overall. Nearly half of the total production of SNJ-4s and T-6Cs had wooden tail sections, but at war's end they were either scrapped, modified or rebuilt into T-6G models

Right Frank Sublett is an ex-Navy Skyhawk pilot who has resprayed his T-6D as an SNJ-5 from the Alameda Naval Air Station. Navy aircraft seem more at home flying over water than over land!

Above Not a scratch to be seen on Bill Dodds' SNJ-5. Even the panel fasteners aren't weathered

Left Post-war, the US Navy continued to decorate their SNJs with a lurid range of contrasting colours, this particular aircraft wearing the markings of an NAS Corpus Christi-based machine. As with the USAAF, the Navy turned the 'Lone Star' state into a land-locked 'carrier' during and after World War 2, much of its flying training taking place over the parched Texan plains. Today, many of those bases established in the war years still churn out ab initio naval aviators

Above The football-shaped housing behind the canopy contained the ADF antenna on early Texans and SNJs. Later models replaced it with a smaller, more compact unit

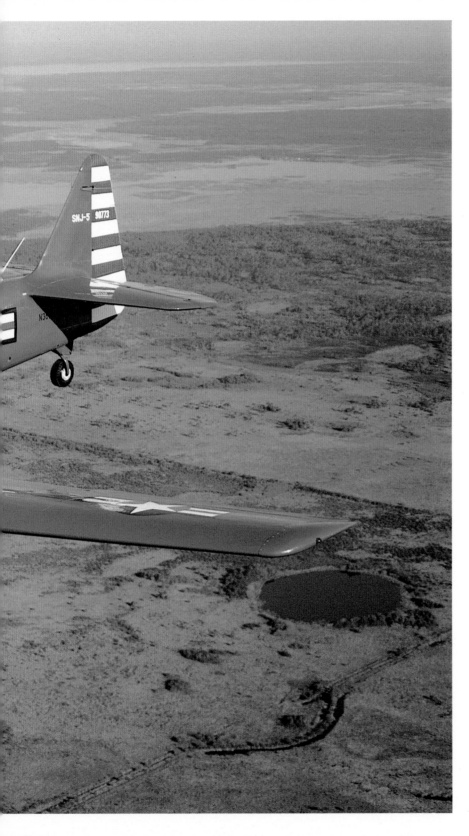

Chuck Clapper flies his SNJ-5 low and slow on an early morning sortie over the Florida countryside. With a cruising speed of about 170 mph, the SNJ is the ideal aerial platform from which to view the landscape

Left Colonel Clapper leads 'his' troops in a formation fly-by over the lush Florida landscape. Sandwiched between the two SNJs are a pair of immaculate T-6Gs. If it wasn't for the varying colour schemes on each aircraft, this photograph could have been taken 40 years ago, the pilots perhaps practising formation flying out of Pensacola or Macdill

Above Two mechanics and a flock of 'technical advisors' strive to repair the starboard oleo leg on this immaculate SNJ-4. A Navy requirement had North American Aviation design and supply a wrench with each SNJ for servicing the aircraft's shock struts

Left The green fuselage band on Walt Ohlrich's SNJ-5 indicates that the aircraft once served as an instrument trainer, whilst the tailcode 'CB' shows that it was based at Corry Field in Florida. Instead of carrying a MODEX number on the fuselage, it wears the aircraft number of the A-4 Skyhawk that Walt flew in Vietnam. Walt's SNJ-5 originally had a wooden rear fuselage assembly but it was modified after the war

Above Under the wing near the landing gear on most SNJs is a small bulb known as a 'bug' light. When the gear was down and locked the light was illuminated, indicating to the carrier LSO (Landing Signal Officer) that the gear was indeed down

Right Jerry Borchin's pristine SNJ-6 leads a gaggle of similar types up to the open door of the C-45 camera ship. Finished in NAS Seattle livery, Jerry's aircraft was winning awards even before it was fully restored

Below Time to flare out at Breckenridge in Marion Gregory's SNJ-5. The US Navy operated the SNJ on training flights until March 1958, whilst the French *Aéronavale* were still flying SNJs up until 1971. The number on the rear fuselage below the tailplane (85077) was the Navy serial or Bureau of Aeronautics Department number (BuNo), a coding system which started in 1911 and is still in use today. Serials have been issued consecutively as required, reaching over 163,000 by 1991

One of the many SNJs that regularly participate in the Confederate Air Force show at Harlingen, this colourful SNJ-5 is finished in the livery of VA-25 'First of the Fleet', embarked on the USS *Midway* (CV-41). During the war, aerial gunners trained on the T-6 at Harlingen, the now famous warbird haven being just another military base in those days

Right A variation on the canopy theme. The earlier model SNJ-3s and -4s had a forward folding rear canopy section, this being changed to the framed, non-folding, style on the SNJ-5, and followed by a one piece clear bubble on the SNJ-6. The one thing that they all had in common was that they leaked, despite years of trying to find a solution!

Above All reserve units had an international orange band around the rear fuselage of their SNJs, with the Naval Air Station code letter painted on the vertical stabilizer and upper starboard and lower port wings. The MODEX on the nose was usually the last three digits of the Navy serial number, but in this case it is the last three numbers of the aircraft's civil registration

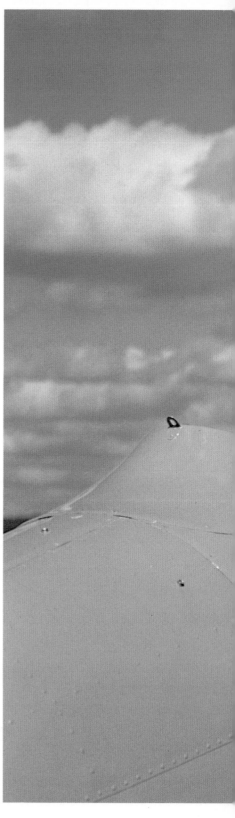

Right The Pratt & Whitney R-1340-AN-1 in Gerry Miles' T-6G. Not the most economical of engines, the '1340 can burn anything up to 40 gallons of fuel per hour, depending of course on how the aircraft is being flown at the time. Like most radial engines, the R-1340 also uses a lot of oil, either burned or leaked. With their aircraft capable of guzzling oil at the rate of a gallon per hour, most SNJ owners have a luggage compartment full of rags at the ready, a ritual wiping of the fuselage taking place soon after landing

Above The round pods under the wings of this SNJ were used to catch spent cartridge shells during its time in service with the Spanish Air Force. Today, these pods are rarely seen on restored airframes

Previous page The Marine Corps, like the Navy, also used the SNJ in large numbers as its basic trainer. Identical to 'blue' SNJs, the USMC aircraft differed only in the titling on the fuselage sides. 'Miss TNT' actually left the North American plant as an AT-6C, the aircraft then being transferred to the 'Corps (*Bob Kennedy*)

Above Although the venerable SNJ could never be described as an awesome fighting machine, fitting a Browning M2 .30 calibre gun just ahead of the cockpit increased the aircraft's 'bite' somewhat. It also helped a budding fighter pilot come to terms with firing a weapon in a 'mock' combat situation, the muzzle flash literally staring him in the face every time he fired the weapon

Right Dan Caldarale is a member of the *Six of Diamonds* formation team, this slick outfit performing at airshows across America. He is a commercial painter by trade and the finish on his aircraft, shown here on the wet grass runway at Geneseo, is a fine example of his craft

Above Although this aircraft was built as an SNJ-5, at some point in its life the original canopy has been replaced with a lightly framed SNJ-6 transparency to enhance the view from the cockpit. The highly polished finish on this aircraft indicates that it has only recently been resprayed

Right Colonel Clapper's SNJ-5 has its original canopy firmly in place, although the highly polished spinner would have been added to the aircraft after it left Navy service. Although the SNJ still has the trough and breach bulge for the Browning gun, Clapper has opted to leave his aircraft weaponless

Right The shade of yellow used on this SNJ-7 is rather more orange than perhaps it should be. This aircraft is actually a T-6G, but because there is little difference between a Texan and a later model SNJ, its owner has opted to paint it up as a Marine Corps machine. The Air Force updated a total of 2068 Texan airframes, re-designating them as T-6Gs, and the Navy embarked on a similar programme to modernize its SNJ fleet. However, only six were completed before the project was cancelled, thus making the last model SNJ as rare an aircraft as the first

Below 'Turn down the volume!' Guaranteed to wake up the neighbours (in another state), 13 SNJs/T-6s run up before taxying out to perform a stirring routine at an airshow in Florida. I would hate to be footing the fuel and oil bill for this line-up

Above Flanked by a P-47D on one side and a P-51D on the other, the 'Pilot Maker' dries out after weathering an autumn sun shower at Chino. Part of the burgeoning fleet of World War 2 types owned by the Planes of Fame organization, this SNJ-5 performs a task not too dissimilar to the one it fulfilled in the war—that of basic trainer for the museum's warbird pilots

Left There is a close resemblance between this wing design and that of the trend-setting Douglas DC-2. The two outer panels, constant chord centre section, flap design, wing sweep and dihedral are identical to that featured on the early Douglas transport. A brief look into the aviation history books solves this seemingly remarkable coincidence however; the designers of the NA-16, James Kindelberger and Lee Atwood, both had careers at Douglas before joining the North American Aviation Company

Left The 'birth certificate' of a R-1340 Wasp radial engine. This plate offers a basic resume of vital engine statistics, acting as a quick visual ready-reckoner for the pilot or the mechanic. The history of the powerplant can be traced from this plate as well, the manufacturer's number mirroring the serial stamped into the reduction gear cover

Above A total of 2198 SNJ-5s were built to US Navy contract at the Dallas factory, the first aircraft being delivered during the summer of 1943. The period markings applied to this aircraft are technically correct for a 1943/44 SNJ, but the pilot's headgear is definitely non-standard issue!

Variations on the theme

Below Somewhat different from the basic Texan, the North American P-64 was built as a fighter for the government of Thailand. Given the model number NA-68, six aircraft were built, crated and shipped as far as Hawaii before a White House arms embargo to war zones came into effect. The single-seat fighters were despatched back to California, stripped of their 20 mm cannon and 8 mm machine guns, and diverted for use by the USAAF. Today, only one of these aircraft is left, owned by Paul Poberenzy, president of the Experimental Aircraft Association. However, several two-seat replicas have been built from Texan airframes flying on the warbird circuit

Left The NA-68 (P-64) was powered by an 870 hp Wright R-1820-77 which drove a three-bladed Hamilton Standard propeller. This engine gave the single-seat pursuit aircraft a top speed of 295 mph, the first NA-68 taking to the skies on 1 September 1940. The delivery of six NA-68s to the Thai Air Force would have undoubtedly increased the effectiveness of their air arm, although what half a dozen trainer-cum-fighters could have done against innumerable Mitsubishi A6M Zeros and Nakajima Ki-43 Oscars is open to question

Right The last variant of the basic design to still have a fixed landing gear, the BT-14 was built for the Army but became primarily an export model. France was the first customer, ordering 230 aircraft (designated NA-57s) in 1939. A follow-on contract for another 230 NA-64s, powered by the slightly different Pratt & Whitney R-985-25 engine, was also placed at the same time, and like the NA-57 order, many airframes had been delivered when France fell to the Germans in June 1940. However, the 119 still being completed back in the USA were immediately snapped up by the RCAF, these aircraft joining the 16 surviving NA-57s that had also failed to be delivered. Designated Yale Mk 1s, they performed tirelessly throughout the war years

Below Looking very much like a Harvard, this Yale wears the markings of No 6 SFTS at RCAF Station Dunnville, Ontario. Many of the NA-57s and -64s that had been delivered to the French went on to train Luftwaffe and Vichy pilots at bases throughout the occupied country until a lack of spares grounded the fleet in 1942

Overleaf The RCAF Yales were powered by a 420 hp Wright R-975-E3 which turning a constant speed propeller, the 'Canucks' further modifying the exhaust system to accept heat muffs. Dan Linkous' 1939 Yale is finished in the scheme it first wore when obtained by the RCAF, the distinctive *Armée de l'Air* colours being faithfully reproduced. Eventually all RCAF Yales were painted standard trainer yellow

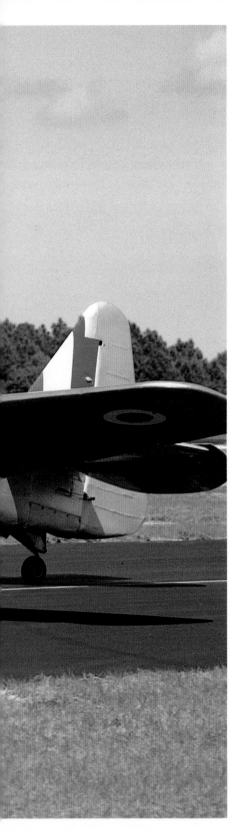

Below At one time a Harvard IV (this airframe was in fact that last one built by the CCF), this aircraft has been modified to look like a North American A-27, a two-seat attack version of the AT-6, built initially for Thailand (as the NA-44). The A-27 was armed with five 0.30 calibre guns; two mounted in the nose; two in the wing; and one in a dorsal mounting. This replica is powered by an R-1820 engine developing 785 hp, and it also has a retractable tailwheel and a shorter wing. Embargoed enroute to Thailand in mid-1940, the A-27s were pressed into service by the USAAC at Nichols Field in the Philippines. All ten aircraft were put out of action during the initial Japanese assault on 8 December 1941, but over the following days they were restored to flying condition and used as scouts and bombers for several weeks before finally being destroyed in action

Left Like many export models, these Yales had instrumentation and placards in the language of the customer. The French Yales were further modified in that their throttle controls were reversed, a backward motion instead of a forward push increasing the power. Linkous is still awaiting a modified exhaust stack for his immaculate Yale

Right 'A6M' Harvards are amongst the most heavily used warbirds on the airshow scene today, getting 'shot down' for the amusement of the paying public across the globe. Be it the Confederate Air Force's Pearl Harbor re-enactment at Harlingen, or the Duxford Fighter Meet's Pacific Air War set-piece over Cambridgeshire, the venerable 'A6Ms' trundle skyward, twist and turn in the gunsights of innumerable Mustangs, Thunderbolts and Corsairs, and finally succumb to the 'hail of shells', streaming smoke to a 'fiery' ending behind a nearby hill. However, unlike 45 years ago, these Zeros return to fight another day

Above Take a Harvard and modify the canopy, the rudder and the cowl, and you have a pretty decent replica of the Japanese A6M Zero for film and television work. Demand from film studios in Hollywood after the war led to the creation of fleets of 'enemy' aircraft built from existing T-6 airframes. This Harvard IV conversion is marked up as the mount of Petty Officer Saburo Sakai, the highest scoring Japanese fighter pilot to survive the War

Left The degree of modification carried out on surplus T-6s can be fully appreciated from this close-up shot, the heavily customized cockpit and canopy being just a small part of the overall rebuilding

Below Smoke systems are popular in warbirds, but are especially effective in Zero replicas. Many 'Zeros' are used in a *Tora, Tora, Tora* routine at airshows, and the smoke adds an air of realism after the aircraft has been 'hit'. Due to its Pearl Harbor notoriety, most A6M replicas are painted in 1941-period naval fighter colours

However, the odd exception to the rule does exist, this beautifully maintained 'A6M' wearing elaborate island camouflage. T-6s were also converted into *Kate* Torpedo bombers for the Hollywood epic *Tora, Tora, Tora,* whilst several Harvards were temporarily modified to resemble P-47 Thunderbolts and Hawker Typhoons for the 1978 film, *A Bridge Too Far*

What do you do when you want to restore an NA-50 and there are no airframes available? Bill Klaers used an SNJ-4 airframe to build one of the most authentic NA-50 reproductions now flying. Features like the original lowered canopy and a flat bottom rudder have all been faithfully reproduced

Above The original NA-50s were built specifically as fighters, and not as armed trainers. Besides the six airframes ordered by Thailand, seven NA-50s were sold to Peru, these aircraft seeing combat during a brief, but bloody, border war against Ecuador in 1941. During the conflict a single NA-50A was downed by enemy ground fire, this aircraft gaining the distinction of being the only one of its type lost in combat. Pete Vandersluis also owns a T-6 painted in the markings of one of the aircraft he flew in the 1950s

Above Pete Vandersluis, who has spent most of his life flying T-6s as a civilian instructor for the Air Force, owns this NA-50 replica, built around a Harvard IV airframe. A 1340AN-2-61 powerplant, with a 12:1 blower enclosed in an ex-Lockheed Constellation cowl, develops about 825 hp, and turns a three-bladed prop that once belonged to a de Havilland Otter

Right The famous USAAC roundel, as worn by the P-64 once the aircraft was pressed in to service at Luke Army Air Base in Arizona

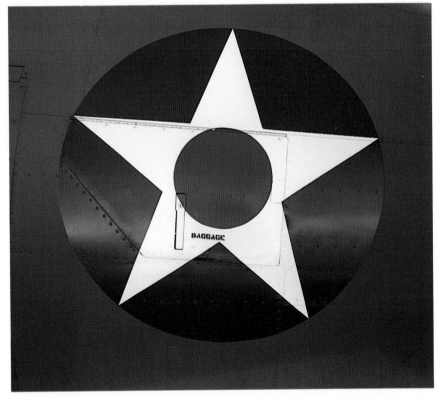

Taxying by at the Valiant Air Command airshow in Florida is 'Miss Sarah', an NA-50 conversion built for Dan McCue by George Baker. Converted from a Harvard airframe, the aircraft has been well received at many east coast airshows, and is now impressing crowds on the west coast as well

The Commonwealth Aircraft Corporation in Australia built a version of the Texan called the Wirraway, the aircraft serving as both a trainer and a scout/fighter. A rugged aeroplane, armed with two .303 Vickers machine guns in the nose and a single flexible mounting for the observer, a Wirraway from No 4 Army co-operation squadron, based in Papua New Guinea, actually shot down an A6M Zero in December 1942. George Baker, who has a love for Australian aircraft, decided to convert his stock Harvard IV into a 'hybrid' Wirraway replica. Like the original, Baker's aircraft is powered by a Pratt & Whitney R-1340-61, his slick creation being finished in Royal Australian Navy colours